Business is Business:
Strictly Financial

MARKUS D. EPTING

NOTE TO READER

Let's just cut to the chase. Years ago, it was expected that employees develop relationships with their employers, but times have changed. Loyalty in the workplace is not as high of a priority as it once was, and the road to success is slightly altered. Business is business. It's strictly financial.

This book is intended to be a 21st century road map to success. Success isn't easy, but no one ever said it had to be difficult. Getting there is easier than you think…

The author has included some humor, but the message is real.

The author is a scientist, an engineer, a businessman, and philanthropist. Employers and affiliates of the author are not credited to this text.

CONTENTS

INTRODUCTION

Knowledge is and has always been a tool for use, but its usefulness
rests in the ability to apply it practically.

I'm reminded of an event in my life as a student. I struggled with
an assignment to create a computer program that turned lights
on and off at various intervals. My roommate walked into the
room. He reeked of marijuana and cheap liquor. He asked to
borrow my car. I cautiously handed him the keys. "I'll be back in
an hour," he said, "assuming I don't run into heavy traffic."
Immediately it hit me. I had been given an assignment to create a
program that modeled a traffic light. Without even knowing it
my roommate had given me the answer, not just to a single
problem but to all life's problems.

During the span of my career I have been fortunate to have shared
space with some very brilliant minds. However, many of those minds
suffered from the ability to transition from theory to application.
Others suffered from lack of preparation.

College graduation is characterized by a feeling of accomplishment
that gives birth to a false sense of entitlement known as the "show
me the money syndrome." Uncertainty follows soon after as
employers aren't lining up take grabs at recent graduates.

To an entry level employee hard work seems more like punishment
for a job well done. Reward and recognition is given at the executive
level and scarce notice is given to the tiny little worker bee. Strategy
becomes a more convenient tool than hard-work, and loyalty takes a
backseat.

Monotony gives rise to a power struggle between the need to
conform and a desire to stand out (individuality). Individuals begin to
question their own abilities to reach the next level. Goals seem even
father from reach. Should you switch jobs maybe even careers ?
Afraid of the risk fear leads to frustration.

1 CONQUERING FEARS

"She has no idea what she's doing in college. The major that she majored in doesn't make any money. She can't drop out. Her parents will look at her funny. Tell me that's not insecure. The concept of school seems so secure. She been a sophomore for 3 years. She still hasn't picked a career." – Kanye West

Okay, maybe that was a little shallow. This quote was obviously borrowed from one of the great lyricists of the 21st century. It's a crude metaphor for "lack of preparation". Success begins with developing and maintaining a life plan, and that means clearly identifying where you are right now, at this very moment, and knowing your purpose for being there. Your purpose for being there should support where you want to go.

Most of us begin drafting our life plan during our adolescent years, and it changes several times throughout puberty and even into college. We start out with dreams of being a ballerina, a wrestler , an

1

actor, an athlete, or an Indian chief, etc. It later develops into something more realistic based on our likes, dislikes, and/or physical abilities. Although you may not have a solid plan by freshman year of college, it's expected that you have a fairly good outline. Late bloomers suffer from a lack of commitment that stems from a fear of failure. Not making a decision means there is zero accountability. How can you fail if you don't try? Temporary security underneath the blanket only leads to regret later in life.

The solution to this problem is realizing that the fear is as real as you and I, but the basis for the fear is not. Understanding that there is no competition in college is the greatest weapon to overcoming fear. Identify your own goals. Recognize that you are in control, and set goals that make sense to you. Choose a path that's conducive to your lifestyle or the lifestyle you want to live. Remember that college is an investment. Try not to incur a massive amount of debt in pursuit of a career that offers a minimal return on your investment, but don't forget to have fun.

The 2nd most important weapon is "time" and learning how to manage it. A little each day goes a long way. Remember there is no competition so feel free to set your own pace, but execute according to the timeline you've set forth. Moving fast in the right direction is not as important as moving in the right direction. Time management will be a tool that, if mastered correctly, will carry you throughout

2

your career. Not to mention, it will do wonders for your confidence.

Rule of thumb: Never miss an assignment, and never miss a party. If you don't feel like homework is a break from all the partying and fun then you probably haven't partied enough.

2 GETTING EMPLOYERS TO NOTICE YOU

More than 40% of recent US college graduates are unemployed. A poll shows that recent graduates often find jobs that don't require a college degree.

What do I do after college?

The answer to this question actually begins during the last semester of college in the months leading up to graduation. The simple answer is flood the market with resumes, but a more tactical approach begins with fully developing the resume (if you haven't already).

If you doubt the strength of your resume it's probably a safe bet that your resume isn't up to par. Hard truth: If it doesn't pass the sniff test it's probably bullshit. But that's okay. Building a really great resume begins with first identifying which types of jobs you want to apply for.

Monster and Indeed are great resources, but let's face it there is heavy traffic on these websites. Oftentimes individuals are contacted by recruiters and not by Human Resources directly. This just adds another layer to the hiring process and increases the wait. A better approach to using Monster and Indeed is to identify which companies are hiring. Then, go directly to that companies website, and begin the application process there. Remember that you will be applying for a huge number of jobs. There is a good chance that you will forget what you've applied for so make a list that will enable you to quickly recall to memory the job announcements long after the posting has been removed.

This next step is critical. Job announcements can be scary as if written by a Ph.D. graduate. Don't let this deter you. Mainly it's a lot of fancy words on a page. The trick is to develop your resume so that it almost mirrors the job description in the job announcement. A simple cut and paste won't do. Use some savvy. This tactic works for one basic reason: HR personnel are usually the first to receive your resume. HR has limited knowledge of what the job responsibilities actually are for the job posting. For instance, a HR person with a business degree has very little knowledge regarding the roles and responsibilities of say, an engineer. A lot of qualified resumes get tossed to the side simply because they aren't well written. If HR has to second guess whether or not you meet the minimum requirements there's a good chance you will never be interviewed. Be neat. Make sure your resume is aesthetically appealing regardless of content.

A lot of job requisitions require experience with particular types of software. Some software is proprietary, but oftentimes it is not. YouTube is a great source for learning how to use new software. Bottomline: If you can learn to play Xbox and PlayStation you can learn how to use a new software tool. Watching a tutorial on YouTube doesn't make you an expert, but it at least gives you some exposure. Now you can take credit for having knowledge of the software, and your resume looks great! Apply and submit.

Congratulations, you've completed Round 1!

3 THE 17TH HOUR

You've developed a fairly solid resume, and odds are you're a good candidate for hire, but let's face the facts. There's only one job opening available, and you're not the only qualified candidate that applied. Recall the list of jobs that you created during Round 1. There's a good chance that there will be similarities between all the jobs contained in the list. However, no one requisition is alike, and the goal is to create a resume that almost mirrors the job announcement. This means you will need a separate resume for every job in the list. Five hundred jobs means 500 resumes so get crackin! With any luck there will only be minor editorial changes.

Running out of time?

Unfortunately for us there are only 24 hours in a day. If you're like most people you only use 16 of them leaving an additional 8 hours for sleep. The remaining 16 hours is stuffed with life events, exams, a part-time job, and an occasional recreational activity. By now though you are an expert at time management. You've been handing over deliverables and meeting deadlines throughout your college career. Squeezing in an extra hour shouldn't give you too much heartburn.

What happens in the 17th hour changes the tempo of the game.

There's less traffic after dark which means you can move faster, maneuver better, and cover more ground in less time. With only minor editorial changes to an already solid resume you should be able to apply for a minimum of 3 jobs within the hour. In the span of a week you've applied for 21 jobs with very little effort. Over the course of a month that's a little over 80 jobs. By then a few phone calls should start rolling in so give yourself a week long break. Then, dive right back in. Now that you've been noticed you can choose to be a little more selective in your job hunt, but there's still the issue of how to champion the interview.

Don't get overconfident just yet, but celebrate a little. You deserve it. A few bottles of champagne won't hurt.

4 CHAMPION OF THE INTERVIEW

I won't advise you on what kind of tie to wear or whether a suit is appropriate or not. I'll leave that up to you, but I can show you how to pass any interview in a few simple steps.

The hardest kind of interview is a behavioral based interview mainly because people aren't prepared for the questions they are about to be asked. If you are an experienced professional you will most likely need to discuss the following areas in some detail, but if you're a new college graduate with limited experience employers will typically give you a hypothetical scenario and ask you to describe how you would handle a particular situation.

Safety:

Employers focus heavily on a safety conscious work environment. When given a scenario such as this you should always answer on the side of conservatism. Why? You may not think so, but you're the low man on the totem pole, and the company would never ask you to make high-risk decisions that could impact profits or create negative press.

Generic Answer: The company has policies and procedures created to handle this kind of situation. If employed one of my first actions would be to familiarize myself with the organization's processes to address the situation accordingly.

There is always the chance that an employer will counter. Don't worry. He or she is just testing you. If the scenario he/she described is beyond the scope of company policy simply reply, "I will seek guidance from more experienced personnel."

Communication:

Scenarios regarding communication are easy.

Generic Answer: Email is not the preferred form of communication. Face to face interaction is always best, but it's definitely a good idea to document important issues.

Obviously the employer understands that face to face interaction is not always feasible. A phone call followed by a verification email is appropriate for important decisions.

Business Execution:

Business execution can be a tough topic to discuss. It really depends on what position you plan to hold in the company. Since you are a recent college grad the following default answer should work.

Generic Answer: Respect for the individual is a basic behavioral principle. Customers, colleagues, associates, and clients should always be treated with dignity and respect regardless of position. I recognize that as an employee of the company I am a representative of the organization and not the voice of the corporation.

Teamwork:

Working in teams can be difficult because of the different personality types. Introverts and extroverts often clash unintentionally. No worries. Be savvy.

Generic Answer: A support role can be just as effective as a leadership role in certain situations. I'm comfortable with both roles. A project lead on one project isn't necessarily a project lead on the next project.

The employer will undoubtedly love this response because it shows humility, and it shows that you recognize your weaknesses and your strengths. Let's face it. No one person is good at everything. This shows integrity. Pat yourself on the back because you're winning!

Time Management:

Lean back in your chair for this one because you already know the answer. You've spent your entire college career drafting the perfect response. Your future employer is likely to give you a scenario dealing with deadlines and a heavy workload. The deadline is approaching, and there is a risk that you will exceed the cutoff date. The answer to the question is a combination of communication and time management.

Generic Answer: As soon as I become aware that I am in jeopardy of not meeting the scheduled deadline I would explain the cause of the delay directly to management. Ideally, management will give me a better understanding of the consequences associated with exceeding the deadline. Being proactive and addressing the issue ahead of schedule enables me to request additional resources or personnel, request overtime, or ask for an extension.

Shake hands after the interview. Send a thank you email to the hiring manager about 5 days letter. Inform him/her that you appreciated a well-organized interview and that you look forward to hearing back soon.

Congratulations! You just landed your first job.

5 SOCIAL MEDIA

We live in the 21ˢᵗ century, and social media is a 'Big Deal.' If you want to be a Rock Star at night go for it. Just don't invite your employer to the concert.

Social media is a great way to stay in touch with friends and family, but it can make or break a career . More often than not it will break you. Keeping your personal life and work life separate is always a safe bet. You won't get a promotion because your employer liked the shirt you wore on Saturday night, but he/she might develop a perception of you based on it. Remember that a person's perception is also their reality, fact or fiction.

Social media sites are a great place to play or promote individual businesses. It is not a place to promote your employer's business unless of course your job is to promote your employer's business. It's certainly not a place to keep in touch with colleagues. For most people 8 hours per day, 5 days a week is more than sufficient time spent with co-workers. I'm not saying you can't befriend your colleagues on social media, but recognize the risk. Social media offers world-wide exposure into your love life, your family woos, and often-times finances. If you wouldn't feel comfortable posting it on the front page of the New York Times then chances are it shouldn't be out on the web. Exposure isn't necessarily always your fault. Friends can tag you in unflattering photographs and ex-boyfriends/girlfriends can post damaging comments about your character. Intentional or unintentional, your friends probably have a lot less to lose than you do.

Twitter, Facebook, and Instagram all offer privacy settings. If you find it necessary to have a social media page you should also be equally responsible for adjusting your privacy settings. Text messaging and phone calls work best when conversing with close friends.

6 THE NEW GUY

Ambition is priceless. You can always identify the 'New Guy' by the glimmer in his eye.

You've just landed your first job. The pay isn't so great, but you're a hard-worker, and in a few years you'll be the CEO, right? Wrong!

There is absolutely nothing wrong with being ambitious. Everybody feels they have something to prove at first. Normally, it's a little bit more apparent in the new guy. Volunteer for the harder assignments, work 50 or more hours per week, and in 3-5 years you are guaranteed to be burnout. With each new assignment your boss gives you a pat on the back and a well-done speech followed by more work. More work in exchange for hard work? That seems more like a punishment than a consolation prize.

Why does this happen?

Hard-work builds character. In due time you become a subject

15

matter expert. Your boss begins to rely on you heavily for assignments mainly because he/she knows the work will get done, and the quality of the work will meet his/her standards. The problem is you probably don't tag along when your boss goes to executive board meetings. You solve all the problems so your boss has all the answers, and he/she receives all the credit. Your boss gets promoted, and it's only fair that you be his/her successor, right? Wrong!

In chess, moving the pieces on the board doesn't necessarily mean you're winning the game.

Remember, you're the new guy, and tenure plays an important part in leadership. The senior guy on the team gets the position because he's more experienced. You're still left doing all the work. I feel your pain. Strategy is the name of the game. Strategy won't be taught in any training program, and you won't find it in any textbook so listen closely.

When you landed the job your employer probably handed you a list of objectives for the year. Focus your efforts on meeting those objectives and those objectives only. Focus only on the tasks you've been assigned. This approach works for two reasons:

1- There is little reward in over-achievement if your boss does not recognize the significance of the achievement. Don't assume he/she does. Most likely all of the additional assignments you volunteer for will be team assignments.

16

When the boss tells you, "Job well done", chances are he/she isn't recognizing any individual achievement. He/she is recognizing your involvement on the **team**.

2- Your own expectations become more realistic.

Additionally, your employer also had you create a 3-5 year Individual Development Plan. Odds are you came up with a plan that would make you Director overnight, and your boss signed off on it.

Get over it!

Your boss was simply satisfying the requirement he was given. An Individual Development Plan is a tool company's use to identify their most ambitious employees, but most companies do not have a policy for enforcing it. So once again your expectations become more realistic. There is less room for disappointment and even lesser room for self-doubt.

So is that it ? Just give up? Is that the answer? Absolutely not!

7 SUCCESS

If an artist gave you an easel and asked you to paint a picture of success it would probably be a vivid array of colors.

This is true of most people, but imagine if you stripped that painting of all its colors. What's left would be an unfinished sketch, black and white. Remember it's your painting, and in order to finish the sketch you have to draw the line somewhere. Where you draw the line is entirely up to you.

If you get excited over titles and fancy office space then you're probably an individual that likes to compete. You can handle the disappointments of being passed up for promotion. You really enjoy the game. You're self-motivated. You have what it takes, and there's no doubt that you will be successful.

But what if you don't care about titles?

If you don't care about titles and your view of success is a nice house

18

and an even nicer bank account then maybe you don't need to compete.

In the 3-5 years that you've been working you've picked up some really cool tools and developed a fairly strong resume, and that's pretty freakin awesome! You've also developed a lot of confidence that employers like to see in young talented individuals, but you're still underpaid, and that can be frustrating. Furthermore, employers are less likely to promote from within because promotions from within usually mean the company also has another slot to fill, your old one. Your greatest advantage in this scenario is your ability to transition. In other words **choose** not to compete. Stop waiting on the promotion. A temporary job change isn't necessarily a bad idea.

In the early stages of your career employers like to see an employee that has been exposed. It's not uncommon for employees to have held 2-3 different jobs in the first 10 years of their career. It shows that you can adapt and learn new tools. The best part is each job change comes with a substantial raise. You already have a job so there's no need for haste. You can even be selective in the employers you choose, but in any case set a monetary goal.

For me the target was a minimum of 10K and not a penny less. In 10 years that's 30K at least, not including annual raises. Not too shabby. With a little luck and some savvy you can even double your income in a matter of years. Changing jobs is a science not an art. It has to make sense. In order for you to realize your new earnings you must factor in cost of living adjustments and taxes. Don't worry if you get low balled by employers. Expect it. There are 2 ways companies make money, earning it and saving it. Naturally an employer wants to hire the best person for the least amount of money possible. There's always wiggle room in negotiations. So if the company offers you a 10K raise ask for 15K.

Okay, I admit it. There's a lot of uncertainty with changing jobs, but making an informed decision is not as hard as it seems. Publicly traded companies issue quarterly and annual earnings statements as well as periodic publications regarding investments and acquisitions. You can locate these online rather easily. If the company is financially sound, then you shouldn't fear making the transition. It's no different from when you landed your first job except now you're a little closer to your hopes and dreams.

It's oftentimes harder to land jobs in glamorous locations. Remember that we've chosen not to compete. Accepting a job in a remote location can earn you alot of extra money without competing with a huge number of other candidates. More disposable income means more purchasing power, freedom to travel and do the things you love, and ultimately financial independence. The job change doesn't have to be permanent as long as it gets you closer to your goal. Once you're satisfied with your earnings then you can focus on longevity with a single employer or maybe even starting your own business. The bottom line is simple, if you're not happy with your earnings you're not going to be happy with your career.

8 THE ROLE OF THE WORK WE DO

Retirement is a time for doing what we love. Most people don't love what they do.

People choose certain careers for various reasons, but most people aren't overly in love with the work they do. Let's face it. Most people aren't exceptionally great at the things they love to do, or at least they're not good enough at it to make any real money doing it. Don't allow the love of the sport to deter you from making the right career choice. The work we do affords us certain lifestyles for ourselves and/or our families.

Your career is moving in the right direction. Take the time to celebrate. Celebration is a time to enjoy all of the things we love. So celebrate often. Remember to save a little now and enjoy alot because retirement is a time to celebrate even more.

9 LETTER FROM THE AUTHOR

Readers and fans alike:

I landed my first job 3 months prior to graduation, and it felt amazing. I couldn't believe that I would be working for NASA. Then the newness wore off, and I realized the money wasn't so great. I bounced from job to job for several years after that. I gained some exposure in the nuclear power industry and even joined the US Missile Defense Agency. Still I wasn't happy. I mean don't get me wrong. My work made for some really great conversations, but I wanted more. It didn't take long for me to realize that there were a huge number of options available to me that I hadn't even considered. I no longer cared about fancy office space and titles because to me success was defined differently. My definition of success was freedom from debt, and that meant dollars.

I've given you some useful tools to help build your career, and hopefully your career will be just as rewarding as I feel mine has been. The greatest gift in life is realizing that you have the strength to remove all obstacles, and that starts with first recognizing that your biggest obstacle is YOU. Fear and doubt can all be overcome with practical approaches to life and all its calamities.
I hope you dream in color.

ABOUT THE AUTHOR

Markus Epting was born on August 3, 1983. Markus is a graduate of the University of Mississippi (Ole Miss) in Oxford, MS and also a graduate of the University of Alabama in Tuscaloosa, AL. He has made notable contributions with the National Aeronautics and Space Administration (NASA), the nuclear power industry, and Missile Defense none of which are accredited to this text. The author is a scientist, an engineer, a businessman, and philanthropist.

www.ingramcontent.com/pod-product-compliance
Lightning Source LLC
Chambersburg PA
CBHW021450170526
45164CB00001B/455